ISBN: 9781670472717

Imprint: Independently published

Published by Civin Media Relations
www.civinmediarelations.com

Printed in the United States

If Every Day Was A Daisy Day

Written by Todd Civin

Illustrated by Eva Anziano

Cavalier Tales
@cavalier_tales

Dedication

*This book is dedicated in loving memory of my mom,
who continues to inspire me every day. It is because of her that I
decided to do therapy dog work with Daisy.
And to my dad. You are my superhero!*

Sandy

There's a saying I heard quite long ago,
I recall it, oh so well.
It may have been a foreshadow,
Of the story I'm about to tell.

"Dogs have a way of finding those,
Who are feeling hurt or sad.
And fill an emptiness inside,
We didn't know we had."

The Cavalier King Charles Spaniel,
Hails from Britain's highest royalty.
Combining gentleness and an athlete's traits,
With grace and loyalty.

Destined to be a therapy dog,
Who we've come to love like crazy.
Has a sense of calm unparalleled,
And the flowery name of Daisy.

Some say she's like a love sponge,
Soaks up everyone's devotion.
There's not a dog more sensitive,
To everyone's emotion.

She's friendly and so confident.
Loves everyone she meets.
When a student joins the room.
They're the first one Daisy greets.

Might change her name to Doc Daisy,
As she seems to diagnose,
Each slightly stressed out person,
Who needs her touch the most.

Once witnessed an amazing incident,
In a class she sees each week.
When a nearly silent student,
Miraculously began to speak.

"Dais" doubles as a watch dog.
Scares intruders with great fright.
But like so many other dogs,
Her bark's not like her bite.

She attends the university
Where each student she observes,
Is greeted by a tail wag,
As Daisy calms their nerves.

After a late night in the library,
They face the next day dragging,
But seem to catch a second wind,
When Daisy's tail's wagging.

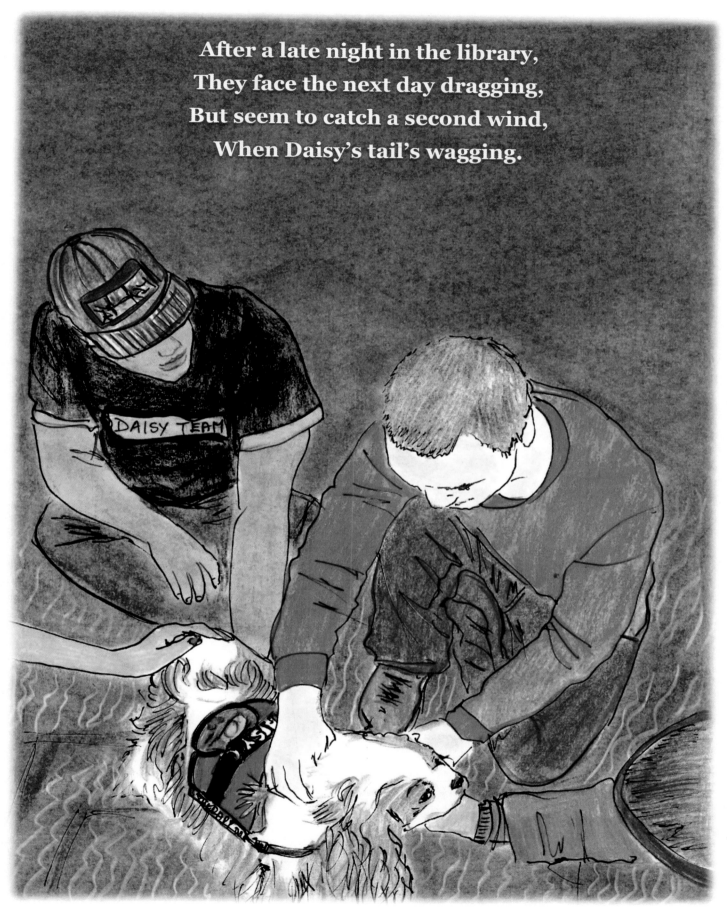

We bring the people coloring pages,
Daisy looks on as they draw.
As if she wants to color too,
Holding crayons with her paw.

The men and women adorned in blue,
Like an officer Daisy's dressed.
An honorary member of the force,
Providing comfort when they're stressed.

When she first showed up in uniform,
It was a rough day for the Chief.
Met Daisy, his new officer,
Who gave him some relief.

She spends time at their open house,
Which really does amuse her.
But there's nothing that she loves quite as much,
As sitting in their cruiser.

Also visits fire houses,
Firefighters can't hide their elation.
Though she cannot ride the fire trucks,
Has less spots than Dalmatians.

On call by day and through the night,
With a heightened sense of urgency.
Ready to provide a dose of love.
In the event of an emergency.

"Dais" also loves the library,
Where she sits in all her glory.
Listens as children read to her,
The words of every story.

When "Daisy Love's" not comforting,
She's certainly not alone.
In fact there are some other dogs,
All chewing on their bones.

In all the home has seven dogs,
With Daisy as the leader.
Bo and Luke and Lola too,
All come from the same breeder.

They're joined by Rocco and Lucy,
They make our house a home.
We'll introduce each one to you,
To finish off this poem.

She's inseparable with
Molly the Rescue dog,
You could tell the way
she kissed her.
It became known as her
"Journey Home."
Turns out Molly
is her sister.

Good Boy Bo, our first Cavalier,
The oldest of the pack.
He could not be a therapy dog,
Has stiffness in his back.

Luke's a star on Instagram,
With tan and white flowing hair.
He has never barked, strong silent type,
You'd hardly know he's there.

If Every Day Was a Daisy Day

Lucy surely barks a lot,
But's in extraordinary health,
She slinks around so cautiously,
Almost invisible   like a stealth.

Rocco's from Hawaii,
Was quite sick at his start,
So filled with love and kindness,
His head has got a heart.

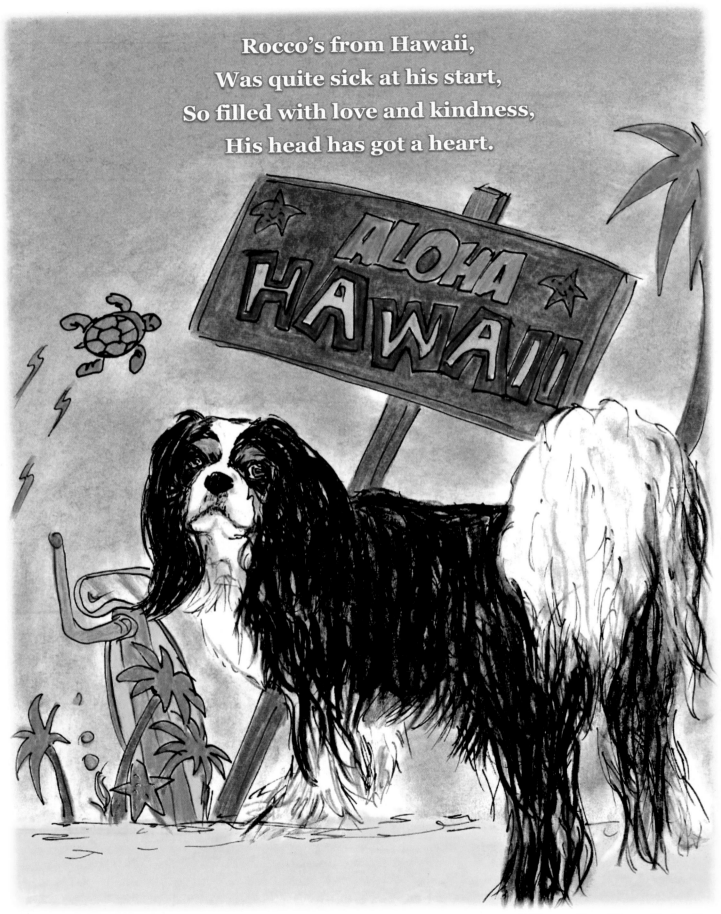

Lola has unruly hair,
The funniest by a mile.
She loves to chew on everything
And make all people smile.

So, if Daisy could speak in human talk,
I'm sure she'd want to say,
Every Day would be so awesome.
If each was a Daisy Day.

Thank You from Sandy and Daisy

Thank you to everyone in my family for your love and support! And, for all your help with Daisy, our other six dogs, an occasional foster, and frequent boarders who seem to just appear out of nowhere, and stay for weeks at a time!

Thank you Barbara (my mentor from Cavalier Rescue USA) for your advice and guidance with all my fosters. Our friendship has grown so much that you've become like a mother to me.

And thank you Heidi, my best friend (and other pea in my pod). Only you can have six dogs of your own and fosters with 9 or 10 puppies, and make it look easy! Thanks for saving all those babies!

Special thanks to Todd and Eva. You are both so incredibly talented! You made one of my dreams a reality, and I am forever grateful!

Thank you to all the officers, firemen, & first responders who spend time with Daisy. The community is a safer place because of people like you!

And, thanks to all the students, staff and wonderful organizations who welcome Daisy into their facilities and their hearts. Daisy loves you all!

Daisy and the rest of the pack can be found on Instagram - @cavalier_tales

A portion of all proceeds from sales of the book will be donated to Cavalier Rescue USA

The Cavalier King Charles Spaniel is a graceful and happy companion, gentle and sweet, yet sporty in character, active and adaptable. In history--known as a "comforter spaniel"--this breed is often just as at ease being an affectionate lap dog as they are taking brisk walks, competing in agility, or fetching a ball many times over.

Cavalier Rescue USA is a national, foster home based, non-profit organization. We are dedicated to finding loving families for Cavaliers who are in need of new homes. The Cavaliers entrusted to us are evaluated for temperament, brought up to date medically, and cared for by our dedicated volunteers until a permanent, loving family is found to adopt them.

Website: cavalierrescueusa.org

Caring People & Sweet Dogs

Sharing Our 4-Legged Friends to Spread Smiles & Joy

Alliance of Therapy Dogs (ATD) provides testing, certification, registration, support, and insurance for members who volunteer with dogs to visit hospitals, special needs centers, schools, nursing homes, and other facilities. We're a network of caring volunteers who are willing to share our special canines to bring smiles and joy to people, young and old alike.

Whether you and your dog are looking to become a certified therapy team or your facility would like to start a therapy dog program, Alliance of Therapy Dogs (ATD) is your #1 choice for pet therapy.

Website: therapydogs.com

Both Stella and Chewy, the inspirations for our brand, were adopted as adult dogs. This inspired our passion for adult and senior pet adoption. Through Journey Home Fund, we raise awareness about the joys of adult and senior pet adoption and donate meals to shelters and rescues across the country who place a focus on this same mission.

https://www.stellaandchewys.com/journey-home/

About the Artist

Eva Anziano is a self-taught artist who resides between Poland and the United States. She is the mother of two children, Dennis, age 10, and Zoë, age 3. Eva specializes in realistic sketches and pyrography. Daisy is her second children's book. There is not much in this world that makes her happier than her children and her artwork. Her work can be found at evaanzianofineart.com or on Facebook at facebook.com/evaanzianofineart

About the Author

Todd Civin is a husband, father of five and grandfather of four to date. He is a graduate of Syracuse University Newhouse School of Public Communications. Todd is the co-owner and creator of Civin Media Relations and is the Social Media Director for the Kyle Pease Foundation and The Hoyt Foundation.

He is the co-author of One Letter at a Time by Rick Hoyt, Destined to Run by Wes Harding, Just My Game by MLB pitcher Jason Grilli, Line Change by Matt Brown and Beyond the Finish by Brent and Kyle Pease. He is also the creator of fifteen children's books among them *Where There's a Wheel There's a Way, A Knight in Shining Armor, A Bike to Call Their Own* and *Together We Finish!*

Created By

@cavalier_tales

Eva Anziano Fine Art

Civin Media
RELATIONS

Made in the USA
Lexington, KY
08 December 2019